Pa
Snowman

by Lisa Torres
illustrated by Diane Paterson

 HOUGHTON MIFFLIN HARCOURT
School Publishers

Copyright © by Houghton Mifflin Harcourt Publishing Company

All rights reserved. No part of this work may be reproduced or transmitted in any form or by any means, electronic or mechanical, including photocopying or recording, or by any information storage and retrieval system, without the prior written permission of the copyright owner unless such copying is expressly permitted by federal copyright law. Requests for permission to make copies of any part of the work should be addressed to Houghton Mifflin Harcourt School Publishers, Attn: Permissions, 6277 Sea Harbor Drive, Orlando, Florida 32887-6777.

Printed in China

ISBN-13: 978-0-547-02898-9
ISBN-10: 0-547-02898-9

11 12 13 14 0940 18 17 16 15 14
4500496268

If you have received these materials as examination copies free of charge, Houghton Mifflin Harcourt School Publishers retains title to the materials and they may not be resold. Resale of examination copies is strictly prohibited.

Possession of this publication in print format does not entitle users to convert this publication, or any portion of it, into electronic format.

"Class, we're making snowmen!"
said Paco's <mark>teacher</mark>, Miss Perez.
"With snow?" asked Paco.
"With scissors and paper," she said.
Miss Perez passed out the scissors.
Paco <mark>studied</mark> his scissors and frowned.

Paco did not like to use scissors.
They just felt strange in his hand.
Paco tried to open and close
the scissors to cut his paper.
But the scissors slipped and slid.
Sometimes they even got stuck.
Paco sighed.

Paco looked at Marisol.
Snip, snip, snip.
Marisol cut a perfect circle
from her white paper.
She used it to make
a snowman's head.

Paco looked at Joshua.

Snip, snip, snip.

Joshua cut a perfect square
from his black paper.

He used it to make
a snowman's hat.

Paco looked at his own paper.
His scissors did not
snip, snip, snip.
His scissors rip, rip, ripped!
Paco's straight lines were not
straight. Paco's curves were
not curved. He sighed again.

Miss Perez walked by Paco's desk.
"What's wrong, Paco?" she asked.
Paco pushed his paper toward
her, then folded his arms. "It
looks like my snowman took a
bite out of his hat!" Paco moaned.
But Miss Perez just smiled.

"I like that idea!" Miss Perez said.

Paco was surprised.

Slowly, he cut another shape.

Its straight lines were not straight.

Its curves were not curved.

He glued it to the snowman's belly.

Miss Perez laughed.
"So your snowman did eat his
hat!" she said.
Paco laughed, too. "Maybe he ate
his carrot nose and buttons, too!"
Paco cut and glued more shapes.

The next day, Miss Perez hung
the snowmen above the fish tank.
They were all round and white,
like polar bears. Except for one.
It had a funny hat and a belly
full of strange shapes. Paco
smiled... and began planning his
next art project.

Responding

✔ **TARGET SKILL** **Compare and Contrast** How is Paco's snowman different from the other snowmen? How is it the same? Make a diagram.

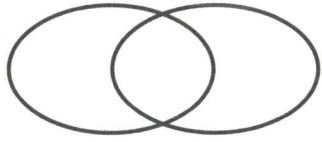

✏ **Write About It**

Text to World Does Paco's snowman look like a snowman you would see in real life? Why? Write two sentences to tell what you think.

above	studied
bear	surprised
even	teacher
pushed	toward

TARGET SKILL **Compare and Contrast** Tell how two things are alike or not.

TARGET STRATEGY **Monitor/Clarify** Find ways to figure out what doesn't make sense.

GENRE **Realistic fiction** is a story that could happen in real life.